# KATHMANDU

## TRAVEL GUIDE 2025

PLUS! COMPLIMENTARY
TRAVEL JOURNAL, CHECKLIST & ITINERARY

# Kathmandu Travel Guide 2025

*Your Indispensable Travel Compass and Companion to Explore and Enjoy KATHMANDU like never before!*

Travel Tips, Tricks & Techniques

Dan L. Allbeta

All rights reserved.

No part of this publication may be reproduced, distributed, or transmitted in any form or by any means, including photocopying, recording, or other electronic or mechanical methods, without the prior written permission of the publisher, except in the case of brief quotations embodied in reviews and certain other non-commercial uses permitted by copyright law.

Copyright © Dan L. Allbeta, 2025

# Table of Content

# PREFACE

I'm happy you took a bold step by investing in this one of a kind travel guide (companion and compass). I hope it will be more than a travel guide and perhaps be a dependable travel companion throughout your stay in and around Kathmandu.

Welcome to the vibrant city of Kathmandu, nestled in the heart of the majestic Himalayas. Prepare to embark on an extraordinary journey filled with ancient history, rich traditions, and breathtaking landscapes.

As you delve into this travel guide, allow yourself to be captivated by the unique allure of Kathmandu, where age-old temples, bustling bazaars, and serene spiritual sites intertwine to create an experience like no other.

Let the adventure begin!

***Dan L. Allbeta***

*"Kathmandu is a city of dreams, a city of magic, a city of mystery."*

***- Pico Iyer***

## Kathmandu a Glance

Kathmandu, nestled in the heart of the majestic Himalayas. As you embark on this remarkable journey through the cultural and natural wonders of Nepal, let us paint a compelling picture of Kathmandu at a glance.

## Diversity of History and Culture

Kathmandu is a city steeped in history, where ancient tales come alive amidst its timeless architecture. Wander through its labyrinthine streets and be transported to a bygone era.

Marvel at the resplendent palaces, adorned with intricate carvings, and discover hidden courtyards that whisper stories of royal dynasties.

The city's rich cultural heritage, deeply rooted in Hinduism and Buddhism, manifests in the myriad temples, monasteries, and stupas that dot the landscape. Each structure is a testament to the devotion and artistic finesse of the Nepalese people.

## The Soul of Spirituality

Kathmandu is a spiritual sanctuary, where seekers of inner peace and enlightenment find solace. Explore the revered Pashupatinath Temple, where the air is thick with the scent of incense and the echoes of sacred chants. Ascend the steps of the Swayambhunath Stupa, known as the "Monkey Temple," and soak in the panoramic views of the city.

## A Place of Colors and Flavors

Kathmandu is a feast for the senses, where vibrant colors and tantalizing flavors entice visitors at every turn. Lose yourself in the bustling markets, brimming with vibrant textiles, intricate handicrafts, and aromatic spices.

Sample the mouthwatering delights of traditional Nepalese cuisine, from the fiery heat of momos to the comforting warmth of dal bhat. Sip on a cup of fragrant chiya (tea) as you engage in lively conversations with locals, who warmly welcome you into their world.

## Nature's Gateway

Beyond the city's captivating streets lies a world of natural splendor waiting to be explored. Kathmandu serves as a gateway to the awe-inspiring Himalayas, drawing adventurers and nature enthusiasts from around the globe.

## A City of Contrasts

Kathmandu is a city of intriguing contrasts, where ancient traditions meet modern aspirations. Witness the harmonious coexistence of temples nestled amidst bustling urban life. Engage with locals, whose warm smiles bridge the gap between cultures and create lasting connections.

Finally, as you delve deeper into the pages of this travel guide, let us unravel the city's hidden gems, provide you with insider tips, and ensure that your experience in Kathmandu is nothing short of extraordinary.

Get ready to be enchanted by the culture, spirituality, and natural wonders that await you in the vibrant heart of Nepal.

*"Kathmandu is a symphony of history, culture, and spirituality, harmonizing in the lap of the Himalayas."*

***- Sudha Shah***

# Chapter 1:
# Historical Antecedent of Kathmandu

Kathmandu, a place where history unfolds like a cherished tapestry. Let's delve into it's rich history and uncover the stories that have shaped this enchanting city.

## Ancient Origins

Kathmandu's history can be traced back over two millennia, to a time when it was a small settlement nestled in the fertile Kathmandu Valley. The valley served as a melting pot of various cultures and ethnicities, with diverse communities finding solace in its serene surroundings. These early settlers laid the foundation for what would later become the vibrant capital of Nepal.

## The Malla Dynasty (12th Century)

In the 12th century, Kathmandu witnessed the rise of the Malla dynasty, which played a pivotal role in shaping the city's cultural and architectural landscape. Under their patronage, Kathmandu flourished as a center of art, trade, and learning.

## Architectural Marvels

Kathmandu is renowned for its architectural marvels that reflect the city's glorious past. The Durbar Squares of Kathmandu, Patan, and Bhaktapur stand as testaments to the artistic prowess of the Malla rulers. These squares, with their palaces, temples, and courtyards, are a living museum of ancient architecture, showcasing exquisite Newari craftsmanship and intricate stone carvings.

## Spiritual Sanctuary

Throughout history, Kathmandu has been a spiritual sanctuary, attracting pilgrims and seekers from far and wide. The city's sacred sites, such as Pashupatinath Temple and Boudhanath Stupa, have been revered for centuries, drawing devotees who seek solace and enlightenment.

These sites are not merely religious landmarks but also cultural touchstones that embody the spiritual essence of Kathmandu.

## Cultural Fusion

Kathmandu has been a melting pot of cultures, where diverse traditions and beliefs intermingle harmoniously. Newars, the indigenous people of the Kathmandu Valley, have played a significant role in shaping the city's vibrant cultural diversity.

Their rich heritage, expressed through festivals, art, music, and cuisine, has become an integral part of Kathmandu's identity, making it a city where cultural fusion thrives.

## A Living Heritage

Today, Kathmandu stands as a living heritage, where the past seamlessly intertwines with the present. Despite the challenges of modernization, the city continues to preserve its architectural treasures and cultural traditions.

Strolling through its narrow alleyways, you will encounter ancient temples, traditional courtyards, and artisans honing age-old crafts.

## The Most Important Historical Events

- **Kantipur (7th century)**

Kathmandu is a city with a long and rich history. The first recorded mention of the city dates back to the 7th century AD, when it was known as Kantipur. The city was founded by the Licchavi dynasty, who ruled the Kathmandu Valley for over 600 years.

- **Malla dynasty (13th century)**

In the 13th century, the Licchavi dynasty was overthrown by the Malla dynasty. The Mallas ruled Kathmandu for over 400 years, and they were responsible for building many of the city's most famous temples and stupas. The most famous of these is the Swayambhunath Stupa.

- **The Gorkhas (18th century)**

In the 18th century, Kathmandu was conquered by the Gorkha kingdom. The Gorkhas ruled Kathmandu for over 200 years, and they made the city the capital of their kingdom.

During this time, Kathmandu continued to grow and develop, and it became a major center of trade and culture.

- **Kathmandu (20th century)**

In the 20th century, Kathmandu was affected by a number of wars and political upheavals. However, the city has always bounced back, and it is now a thriving metropolis. Kathmandu is home to a population of over 1 million people, and it is a major tourist destination.

## 5 Little-known Facts About Kathmandu

Here are the little-known facts about the historical antecedent of Kathmandu:

1. The city was originally founded on a lakebed, and it was once surrounded by a moat.
2. The city was a major center of trade during the Malla period, and it was known for its silk production.
3. Kathmandu was the capital of the Gorkha kingdom from 1768 to 1951.
4. The city was badly damaged by an earthquake in 1934.
5. Kathmandu is now a major tourist destination, and it is home to a number of UNESCO World Heritage Sites.

*"Kathmandu is not just a destination; it's an emotional journey where you discover the beauty of your own soul."*

***- Eric Valli***

# Chapter 2:
# The Best Time Of The Year To Visit

Kathmandu stands as an alluring destination that beckons travelers year-round. However, to truly savor the essence of this enchanting city and its cultural marvels, timing your visit is key.

In this chapter, let us guide you to discover the best time to visit Kathmandu and unveil its myriad wonders.

## Spring: A Blossoming Spectacle

As winter bids adieu to the valley, the arrival of spring paints Kathmandu in a vibrant tapestry of colors.

The months of March to May unveil the city at its finest, with the rhododendrons in full bloom, adding a touch of magic to the landscape.

Temperatures are pleasantly mild, making it an ideal time to embark on city tours and explore the breathtaking cultural heritage of Kathmandu.

## Summer: A Fusion of Festivities

The summer months from June to August embrace Kathmandu in a warm embrace. Though temperatures rise, the atmosphere buzzes with a festive spirit as locals celebrate various cultural events.

The verdant valleys and lush landscapes create a mesmerizing backdrop, enticing nature enthusiasts to take leisurely strolls and experience the city's unique charm.

## Autumn: A Trekker's Paradise

The golden hues of autumn embrace Kathmandu from September to November, making it a true paradise for trekkers and adventure seekers. The clear skies and mild weather provide the perfect conditions for embarking on thrilling hikes and treks, including the iconic Everest Base Camp trek.

Autumn also marks the celebration of lively festivals, offering travelers a chance to immerse themselves in the rich cultural tapestry of the region.

## Winter: A Serene Retreat

As the temperatures dip from December to February, Kathmandu transforms into a serene retreat, shrouded in mist and tranquility. The off-season presents a unique opportunity to explore the city's hidden gems without the bustling crowds.

If you're seeking a peaceful escape amidst snow-capped peaks, winter casts an enchanting spell over the valley.

## Choosing Your Time to Unveil Kathmandu

Kathmandu is a city that can be visited year-round, but there are certain times of year that are better than others for tourists. The best time to visit Kathmandu is during the spring (March-April) or fall (October-November).

Selecting the best time to visit Kathmandu also depends on your preferences and the experiences you seek. Each season offers a distinct charm, be it the blossoming hues of spring, the festive aura of summer, the trekker's delight in autumn, or the tranquil retreat of winter.

## 4 Key Factors To Consider

Here are some other factors to consider when planning your trip to Kathmandu:

- **Festivals:**

Kathmandu is a city that celebrates many festivals throughout the year. If you are interested in experiencing Nepali culture, you may want to plan your trip around one of these festivals. Some of the most popular festivals include Dashain, Tihar, and Holi.

- **Hiking:**

If you are interested in hiking, the best time to visit Kathmandu is during the spring or fall. The weather is mild during these seasons, and the trails are less crowded.

- **Trekking:**

If you are planning on trekking in the Himalayas, the best time to visit Kathmandu is during the spring or autumn. The weather is mild during these seasons, and the trails are less crowded.

*"Kathmandu is a city where the past and present collide, where the sacred and the profane coexist."*

***- Mark Twain***

# Chapter 3:
# How To Arrive and Move Like a Pro

As you prepare to take flight and land amidst the cultural marvels of Nepal's capital, let us guide you on how to arrive and navigate the city like a seasoned traveler.

## Various Mode Of Transport Across Borders

### Airplane

The most common way to get to Kathmandu is by plane. There are many international airlines that fly to Kathmandu, including Nepal Airlines, Buddha Air, and Himalaya Airlines. The main international airport in Kathmandu is Tribhuvan International Airport, which is located about 15 kilometers from the city center.

### Train

There is currently no direct train service to Kathmandu from other countries. However, there is a train service from India that connects to Kathmandu. The train journey from India to Kathmandu takes about 24 hours.

## Bus

There are also bus services that connect Kathmandu to other countries in South Asia. The bus journey from India to Kathmandu takes about 24 hours, and the bus journey from Bangladesh to Kathmandu takes about 36 hours.

## Car

It is also possible to drive to Kathmandu from other countries in South Asia. However, the road conditions can be challenging, and the journey can take several days.

***Which mode of transportation is right for you?***

The best mode of transportation for you will depend on your budget, your time constraints, and your preferences. If you are on a tight budget, then the bus or train may be the best option for you.

If you are short on time, then flying may be the best option for you. And if you want to have a more adventurous journey, then driving may be the best option for you.

## How To Get the Best of Your Arrival

### The Art of Arrival:

Arriving in Kathmandu is an experience like no other, and to truly immerse yourself in its charm, you must first master the art of arrival. As your plane descends, keep your eyes peeled for the breathtaking sight of the snow-capped Himalayan peaks peeking through the clouds.

With the city nestled amidst these majestic giants, the landing itself becomes a preview of the awe-inspiring journey that lies ahead.

Before you land, ensure you have your travel documents and customs forms ready for a smooth transition through the airport.

Once you touch down at Tribhuvan International Airport, a sense of excitement and curiosity will wash over you as you step foot on Nepali soil.

## Navigating Immigration and Customs:

As you enter the airport terminal, follow the signs to immigration and prepare to show your passport and visa. Be patient, as the process may take some time, but the friendly officials will ensure that your entry into Nepal is hassle-free.

Next comes the customs check. Nepal warmly welcomes tourists, but some items may be subject to duty and import restrictions. To breeze through this process, it's essential to be honest and declare any necessary items, ensuring your journey starts on the right foot.

## Finding Your Ground:

With immigration and customs cleared, it's time to retrieve your luggage and set foot into the heart of Kathmandu. As you exit the airport, you'll be greeted by a bustling scene of eager faces, enthusiastic taxi drivers, and a vibrant buzz that defines the city. To get to your accommodation smoothly, prearrange a reliable taxi service or, if your accommodation offers it, an airport pick-up.

Keep in mind that haggling is customary in Nepal, so don't hesitate to negotiate the fare. The ride into the city is an opportunity to take in the sights and sounds, so keep your camera handy!

## Settling in - The Hospitality of Kathmandu:

Upon reaching your accommodation, take a moment to catch your breath and soak in the hospitality of Kathmandu. The city is known for its warm and welcoming locals, and you'll quickly find yourself feeling at home.

Many hotels and guesthouses offer traditional Nepali tea as a gesture of welcome and a delightful treat.

## Navigating the City:

With your base established, it's time to begin your exploration of Kathmandu. The city's winding streets and labyrinthine alleys can be a puzzle, but fear not! Armed with a map and a sense of adventure, you'll soon discover the city's hidden gems.

## Top 4 Tips for Arriving in Kathmandu:

- Be prepared for crowds. Kathmandu is a busy city, and the airport is no exception. There will be a lot of people, so be prepared to wait in line.
- Have your passport and visa ready. You'll need to show your passport and visa to immigration officials when you arrive.
- Know where you're going. If you're not sure where you're staying, have the address written down or saved on your phone.
- Be aware of your surroundings. Kathmandu is a safe city, but it's always a good idea to be aware of your surroundings, especially in the airport.

## Top 7 Tips for Landing in Kathmandu:

- Take your time. There's no need to rush. Take your time getting off the plane and collecting your luggage.
- Be patient. The immigration process can take some time, so be patient and don't get frustrated.
- Use a taxi. Taxis are the most convenient way to get from the airport to your hotel.
- Don't be afraid to ask for help. If you're lost or need help, don't be afraid to ask for help from a local or a hotel staff member.
- Exchange your currency at the airport. You'll get a better exchange rate at the airport than you will in the city.
- Buy a SIM card for your phone. This will give you access to data and make it easier to get around.
- Download a map of Kathmandu. This will help you get around the city and find your way to your hotel.
- Be prepared for the altitude. Kathmandu is located at a high altitude, so you may experience some altitude sickness. Drink plenty of fluids and take it easy for the first few days.

# Chapter 4: Culture and Tradition of Kathmandu

Kathmandu, a city steeped in ancient culture and cherished traditions that have withstood the test of time. As you step into the heart of this mystical destination, prepare to be immersed in a rich diversity of customs, rituals, and celebrations that define the essence of Kathmandu.

## The Spirit of Harmony:

At the very core of Kathmandu's culture lies a spirit of harmony and unity.

Despite its diverse ethnicities and languages, the people of Kathmandu share a deep bond, embracing one another's differences with open hearts.

A unique amalgamation of Hinduism, Buddhism, and other religions creates a vibrant cultural mosaic that colors every aspect of life in the city.

## The Enchanting Festivals:

Festivals in Kathmandu are a collection of colors, music, and devotion, drawing travelers and locals alike into a mesmerizing realm of celebration. From Dashain, the longest and most significant Hindu festival, to the exuberant festival of lights, Tihar, each event is a symphony of traditions that blend spirituality with joy.

During these lively festivities, the city comes alive with processions, dances, and rituals that echo through the narrow streets and ancient temples.

## Temples - Guardians of Time:

Kathmandu is home to a plethora of historic temples, each bearing witness to the city's illustrious past. Durbar Square, a UNESCO World Heritage Site, stands as a testimony to the artistic brilliance of the Newar community. The Taleju Temple, Hanuman Dhoka Palace, and Kumari Ghar are just a few of the architectural marvels that adorn this sacred space.

Among the most iconic is the Boudhanath Stupa, an impressive Buddhist monument that exudes an air of tranquility and spirituality. As you walk around the stupa, you'll be immersed in the soothing chants of Buddhist monks and the fluttering prayer flags that carry the hopes and prayers of countless devotees.

## Art and Crafts - A Timeless Legacy:

The craftsmanship of Kathmandu's artisans reflects a heritage handed down through generations. Intricately carved wooden windows, metalwork, pottery, and colorful thangka paintings grace the markets and temples, showcasing the city's artistic finesse. Be sure to visit the Thamel area, where bustling markets offer an array of exquisite handicrafts and souvenirs that you can take home as precious mementos of your journey.

## Religion:

Religion is a central part of life in Kathmandu. The city is home to many temples and monasteries, and religious festivals are celebrated throughout the year.

## Art and architecture:

Kathmandu is a city of art and architecture. The city is home to many temples, palaces, and stupas, which are all examples of the city's rich artistic heritage.

## Culinary Delights:

Kathmandu's culinary scene is a delight for the senses, boasting a tantalizing array of flavors and aromas. The city's gastronomy is heavily influenced by Tibetan, Indian, and Newari cuisines. Indulge in momos, steamed dumplings filled with succulent meat or vegetables, and savor the traditional Newari feast of dal bhat, a delectable combination of lentil soup and rice.

As the sun sets, the streets come alive with food vendors offering tantalizing snacks like sel roti and chatamari. Don't miss the opportunity to sip on a cup of masala tea as you relax in the warmth of a local teahouse, absorbing the sights and sounds of everyday life in Kathmandu.

## Important Dates and Celebrations in Kathmandu

Here are some of the most important dates and celebrations in Kathmandu:

- **Dashain:**

Dashain is the most important festival in Nepal. It is a 15-day festival that celebrates the victory of good over evil.

- **Tihar:**

Tihar is also known as the Festival of Lights. It is a five-day festival that celebrates the bond between humans and animals.

- **Holi:**

Holi is a festival of colors. It is celebrated by throwing colored powder and water at each other.

- **Maghe Sankranti:**

Maghe Sankranti is a festival that marks the end of the winter solstice and the beginning of the spring equinox.

- **Buddha Jayanti:**

Buddha Jayanti is the birthday of the Buddha. It is celebrated by Buddhists all over the world.

**Here are some additional tips for attending festivals in Kathmandu:**

- **Dress appropriately:** Some festivals have dress codes, so be sure to check before you go.
- **Be respectful:** Festivals are religious and cultural events, so be sure to be respectful of the traditions and customs.
- **Be prepared for crowds:** Festivals can be crowded, so be prepared to wait in line and jostle for space.
- **Have fun:** Festivals are a great way to experience Kathmandu's culture and tradition, so have fun and enjoy the festivities!

*"In Kathmandu, time slows down, allowing you to immerse yourself in the richness of the culture and the beauty of the surroundings."*

***- Elizabeth Hawley***

# Chapter 5:
# Accommodation in Kathmandu

When it comes to finding the perfect place to rest your weary feet in Kathmandu, the city offers a diverse array of accommodations to suit every traveler's taste and budget.

From cozy guesthouses tucked in quaint alleyways to luxurious hotels with breathtaking views, Kathmandu ensures you have a home away from home during your unforgettable journey.

## Hotels:

Kathmandu has a wide variety of hotels to choose from, ranging from budget-friendly to luxurious.

# 5 Best Hotels in Kathmandu

## 1. Aloft Kathmandu Thamel

**Description:** Located in the lively city center, making it a perfect choice for guests seeking relaxation, exploration, and an authentic Nepalese experience. Thamel, known as a tourist hotspot, is just a short distance from UNESCO heritage sites, making it a hub of entertainment and excitement, blending both local and international charm.

**Rating:** 4.6/5.0

**Contact:** +977 1-5252000

**Website:**

https://www.marriott.com/en-us/hotels/ktmal-aloft-kathmandu-thamel/overview/

## 2. Marriott Kathmandu

A modern hotel in the capital city of Nepal, Kathmandu, offering 213 stylish rooms that blend contemporary design with local creativity. The rooms are elegantly decorated with warm colors, exuding a charming ambiance, and our attentive service perfectly complements your stay.

**Rating:** 4.6/5.0

**Contact:** 009 1 844-631-0595

**Website:**

https://www.marriott.com/en-us/hotels/ktmmc-kathmandu-marriott-hotel/overview/

### 3. The Dwarika's Hotel

**Description:** The Dwarika's Hotel in Kathmandu is a true reflection of Nepal's ancient cultural heritage, blending rich Nepali hospitality with exquisite architectural traditions. Originally intended as a heritage restoration project, it has now become Nepal's top property and a role model for heritage preservation in the country and beyond.

**Rating:** 4.6/5.0

**Contact:** (+977-1) 4579488 / 4570770

**Website:** https://www.dwarikas.com/home/

### 4. Hotel Yak and Yeti

Description: Located in the heart of Kathmandu, Nepal, is a luxurious 5-star deluxe hotel. It blends modern sophistication with cultural heritage, featuring a 100-year-old palace and a newly designed structure.

Surrounded by antique fountains, gilded temples, and lush gardens, the hotel offers a serene retreat just moments away from the bustling shops and exciting adventures of Kathmandu city.

**Rating:** 4.0/5.0

**Contact:** +977 1 4248999, 4240520

**Email:** reservation@yakandyeti.com.np

**Website:** https://www.yakandyeti.com/

**5. Hyatt Regency Kathmandu**

**Description:** A luxurious 5-star hotel and resort situated in Kathmandu. The design is inspired by traditional Newari style of Nepalese architecture. This stunning hotel and resort lies on the way to the Boudhanath Stupa, a sacred Tibetan Buddhist shrine outside Tibet and a UNESCO World Heritage Site, which is just a 5-minute walk away.

**Rating:** 4.5/5.0

**Contact:** +977 1 517 1234

**Website:**

https://www.hyatt.com/en-US/hotel/nepal/hyatt-regency-kathmandu/kathm

## Guesthouses:

Guesthouses are a popular option for budget travelers. They are usually small, family-run establishments that offer basic accommodations.

- **Kathmandu Guest House**

It provides budget-friendly accommodation in the popular tourist district of Thamel. The guest house has its own restaurant and offers free private parking. You can access free Wi-Fi throughout the property. Additionally, they offer a complimentary airport pick-up service from the International airport. Kathmandu Guest House is located 7 km from Tribhuvan Airport and Patan Durbar Square.

**Rating:** 4.5/5.0

**Contact:** (+977-1) 470 0632

**Website:** https://ktmgh.com/kathmandu-guest-house/

## Homestays:

Homestays are a great way to experience Nepalese culture. You will stay with a local family and learn about their way of life.

- **Homestay Nepal**

This cozy and welcoming family homestay nestled in the serene countryside of Langol, a mere 10km away from the heart of Kathmandu. It offers modern amenities like western bathrooms, comfortable beds, and free Wi-Fi. As part of your stay, you'll relish a scrumptious home-cooked organic dinner prepared with love from Belku's garden. Don't miss the chance to savor the traditional Newari dish, Dhal Bhat.

**Rating:** 4.5/5.0

**Contact:** +977-9841435773

**Website:** http://www.familyhomestaykathmandu.com/

# 6 Keys to Choose a Suitable Accommodation

Here are the essential keys to help you choose a suitable accommodation in Kathmandu:

## 1. Location

The first key is the location of your accommodation. Consider staying in the heart of Kathmandu's vibrant neighborhoods like Thamel, where you'll find an array of restaurants, shops, and cultural attractions just steps away. If you prefer a tranquil retreat, explore options in areas like Boudha or Nagarkot, offering serene surroundings and breathtaking views of the Himalayas.

## 2. Comfort and Amenities

Unlock the door to comfort and convenience by checking the amenities offered by each accommodation. Look for essential facilities like comfortable beds, clean bathrooms, and Wi-Fi connectivity. Depending on your preferences, you may also desire additional features such as a rooftop terrace, spa, or on-site restaurant for a delightful stay.

### 3. Budget

Your budget is a crucial key in selecting suitable accommodation. Evaluate your spending limit and explore options that match your financial plan. From budget-friendly guesthouses to luxurious resorts, Kathmandu offers a wide range of choices to accommodate various budgets without compromising on quality.

### 4. Reviews and Recommendations

Seek the wisdom of fellow travelers to unlock the door to confidence in your choice. Read reviews and recommendations from previous guests to gain insights into the experience they had at a particular accommodation. This key will help you gauge the level of service, cleanliness, and overall satisfaction of past visitors.

### 5. Cultural Connection

To immerse yourself fully in the cultural tapestry of Kathmandu, consider staying in a guesthouse or homestay. These accommodations provide an opportunity to interact with friendly locals, indulge in home-cooked meals, and experience traditional Nepalese hospitality firsthand.

### 6. Accessibility

When choosing your accommodation, consider its proximity to major attractions, public transportation, and the airport. This key will ensure that you can explore the wonders of Kathmandu without unnecessary travel time, making the most of your precious moments in the city.

In conclusion, choosing a suitable accommodation in Kathmandu is an important decision that can significantly enhance your travel experience. By utilizing these essential keys of location, comfort, budget, reviews, cultural connection, and accessibility, you will unlock the door to a memorable and enriching stay in this captivating city.

Allow these keys to guide you as you unlock the perfect abode to create cherished memories that will linger in your heart for years to come.

*"Kathmandu, a city that teaches you the art of finding beauty in simplicity and grace in imperfection."*

***- Arpana Rayamajhi***

# Chapter 6:
# Must-See Attraction Spots in Kathmandu

As you delve deeper into the heart of Kathmandu, get ready to be mesmerized by its rich history, vibrant culture, and breathtaking landscapes.

In this chapter, we unveil some of the must-see attraction spots that will leave you in awe and create lasting memories of your journey through this enchanting city.

## Swayambhunath (Monkey Temple)

This 500-year-old stupa is one of the most important Buddhist sites in Nepal. It is located on a hilltop overlooking Kathmandu Valley, and it offers stunning views of the city and the surrounding mountains.

Affectionately known as the Monkey Temple due to its playful primate residents, this ancient monument stands as a symbol of religious harmony. As you reach the top, soak in the panoramic views of the city and the majestic Himalayan peaks.

## Patan Durbar Square

This UNESCO World Heritage Site is home to a number of temples, palaces, and courtyards. It is the heart of Kathmandu's old town, and it is a great place to wander around and soak up the atmosphere.

## Pashupatinath Temple

This Hindu temple is one of the most important pilgrimage sites in Nepal. It is located on the banks of the Bagmati River, and it is dedicated to Shiva, the Hindu god of destruction and regeneration.

Prepare for an immersive spiritual journey at Pashupatinath Temple, a revered Hindu pilgrimage site.

Witness the intricate architecture, vivid rituals, and traditional cremation ceremonies that reflect the sacredness of life and death. As you walk through the hallowed grounds, you'll sense the profound spirituality that permeates every corner of this extraordinary place.

## Boudhanath Stupa

This 14th-century stupa is one of the largest in the world. It is located in the Kathmandu suburb of Boudha, and it is a popular tourist destination. Prepare to be humbled by the serene aura of Boudhanath Stupa, one of the largest stupas in the world and a significant pilgrimage site for Buddhists.

## Changu Narayan Temple:

This 1,200-year-old temple is located on a hilltop overlooking Kathmandu Valley. It is a UNESCO World Heritage Site, and it is one of the oldest temples in Nepal.

## Garden of Dreams

Escape the bustling city life and find tranquility in the Garden of Dreams, an enchanting neo-classical garden nestled amidst the urban chaos. The meticulously manicured lawns, lush flowers, and elegant pavilions create a peaceful haven.

Enjoy a leisurely stroll, unwind with a book, or simply savor moments of solitude in this idyllic retreat.

## Enchanting Parks and Gardens in Kathmandu

These verdant oases are like hidden gems, inviting travelers to immerse themselves in nature's embrace. In this section, we will unlock the beauty of these serene havens and help you discover the perfect spots to unwind and rejuvenate.

- **The Garden of Dreams:**

This beautiful garden was built in the 19th century, and it is one of the most popular tourist destinations in Kathmandu. The garden is home to a number of pavilions, fountains, and flowerbeds, and it offers stunning views of the city.

**Email:** info@gardenofdreams.org.np/

**Website:** https://gardenofdreams.org.np/

**Rating:** 4.5/5.0

**Shankhamul Park:**

This spacious garden is adorned with tall trees, creating a refreshing canopy under which you can relax and savor the beauty of nature. Engage in a friendly game of badminton or enjoy a picnic with friends and family, as the park offers a wonderful atmosphere for a delightful day out.

- **Swayambhunath Park:**

This park is located on a hilltop overlooking Kathmandu, and it offers stunning views of the city and the surrounding mountains. The park is home to a number of temples and monasteries.

- **Tulsipur Garden:**

This garden is located in the Kathmandu suburb of Boudha, and it is home to a number of temples and monasteries. The garden is also a popular spot for birdwatching, and it is a great place to escape the hustle and bustle of the city.

- **National Botanical Garden:**

This garden is located on the outskirts of Kathmandu, and it is home to a wide variety of plants and flowers. The garden is a great place to learn about Nepal's rich plant life, and it is a popular spot for picnics and family outings.

- **Ratna Park:**

As the oldest public park in Kathmandu, Ratna Park holds the key to a cherished historical past. Unlock the stories of the city's evolution as you walk along the well-maintained pathways, surrounded by lush vegetation and bright blooms

- **Tribhuvan Park:**

Unlock an urban oasis in the heart of the bustling city at Tribhuvan Park. This vibrant garden welcomes you with neatly landscaped lawns, fragrant blossoms, and playful fountains. Whether you seek a refreshing morning jog or a serene place to read a book, Tribhuvan Park offers a lovely setting to reconnect with nature.

- **Godavari Botanical Garden:**

Unlock the hidden treasures of biodiversity at Godavari Botanical Garden, nestled at the foothills of the Phulchoki Mountain. Home to a diverse collection of flora, including rare plant species.

- **Chandragiri Hills:**

Unlock the wonders of Kathmandu's panoramic beauty at Chandragiri Hills. While technically not a park or garden, this hill station offers a breathtaking view of the valley and the surrounding mountains. A cable car ride to the top unlocks a surreal experience, allowing you to witness the majestic Himalayan peaks that stand tall on the horizon.

*"Kathmandu is a city that awakens your senses and embraces you with its timeless charm."*

***- Pico Iyer***

# Chapter 7:
# Food and Drink

From traditional Nepali delicacies to international cuisines, each dish and beverage holds the key to a delightful and unforgettable dining experience.

## Dal Bhat - The Heart of Nepali Cuisine:

Unlock the essence of Nepali culture with a plate of Dal Bhat, the heart and soul of Nepali cuisine. This wholesome meal consists of steamed rice (Bhat) served with lentil soup (Dal) and a variety of side dishes, such as vegetable curries, pickles, and papadums.

## Momos - The Dumpling Delight:

As you explore the bustling streets of Kathmandu, be sure to unlock the joy of Momos, a beloved dumpling delicacy. These steamed or fried dumplings are filled with succulent meats or vegetables and served with spicy dipping sauces. Whether enjoyed as a quick street snack or a sit-down meal, Momos are sure to tantalize your taste buds.

## Newari Delights - Rich in Tradition:

Indulge in Newari delicacies like Yomari (sweet rice dumplings), Chatamari (Nepali pizza), and Choila (marinated meat). Each bite is a journey through time, unlocking the flavors cherished by the Kathmandu Valley's indigenous community.

## Thakali Thali - A Wholesome Feast:

This set meal typically includes rice, lentils, various vegetable curries, meat dishes, pickles, and yogurt. Thakali Thali showcases the diversity of Nepali flavors, unlocking a harmony of tastes on a single plate.

## Tibetan Specialties - A Cultural Fusion:

Unlock the fusion of Tibetan and Nepali cuisines with Tibetan specialties like Tibetan bread, butter tea, and thukpa (noodle soup). These dishes represent the cultural intertwining of the two regions, offering a unique and flavorsome experience.

## Chai and Lassi - Beverage Bliss:

Quench your thirst and unlock beverage bliss with a steaming cup of chai (spiced tea) or a refreshing glass of lassi (yogurt drink). These quintessential beverages are readily available across the city and offer the perfect way to relax and soak in the vibrant ambiance of Kathmandu.

## International Cuisine - A Global Affair:

Unlock the world on your plate as Kathmandu welcomes a diverse range of international cuisines. From Italian pasta to Indian curries, from Japanese sushi to Middle Eastern falafels, the city's food scene embraces global flavors, offering a culinary adventure for every palate.

In conclusion, Kathmandu's food and drinks hold the key to a culinary journey that unlocks a rich tapestry of flavors and cultural heritage. Whether you explore traditional Nepali delicacies, savor Newari delights, or indulge in international cuisines, each dish and beverage invites you to unlock a delightful and unforgettable experience that will linger in your heart and taste buds long after you depart.

## 5 Must Taste Cuisine in Kathmandu

- **Dal Bhat:** This is the national dish of Nepal, and it is a must-try for any visitor. Dal Bhat consists of rice, lentils, vegetables, and a curry. It is a filling and nutritious meal that is perfect for any time of day.

- **Momos:** These are steamed dumplings that are filled with a variety of ingredients, such as meat, vegetables, or cheese. Momos are a popular street food in Kathmandu, and they can be found all over the city.

- **Thukpa:** This is a noodle soup that is made with a variety of ingredients, such as meat, vegetables, and spices. Thukpa is a popular winter dish in Kathmandu, and it is a great way to warm up on a cold day.

- **Lassi:** This is a yogurt drink that is flavored with a variety of ingredients, such as fruit, spices, or nuts. Lassi is a refreshing and delicious drink that is perfect for any time of day.

## Best 7 Place to Eat in Kathmandu

There are many great places to eat in Kathmandu, but here are a few of my favorites:

- **Newa Lahana:**

This restaurant serves traditional Newari cuisine, which is the cuisine of the Kathmandu Valley. The food is delicious and the atmosphere is authentic.

- **Janakpur Kitchen:**

This restaurant serves Indian cuisine, and it is one of the best places in Kathmandu to get a good Butter Chicken.

- **Dolma:**

This restaurant serves Tibetan cuisine, and it is a great place to try Thukpa or Momos.

- **Everest Kitchen:**

This restaurant serves international cuisine, and it is a great place to find something for everyone.

- **Roadhouse Cafe:**

This cafe is a popular spot for both tourists and locals. They serve a variety of Western and Nepali dishes, and they have a great selection of coffee and tea.

**Contact Number:** +977 9820805958

**Email:** marketing@roadhousenepal.com

**Website:** https://roadhouse.com.np/boudha

- **Mitho Cafe Restro:**

This cafe is a great place to relax and people-watch. They have a variety of snacks and light meals, and they have a great selection of coffee and tea.

**Rating:** 4.5/5.0

- **Northfield Cafe and Jesse James Bar:**

This cafe is a great place to grab a bite to eat and enjoy a drink. They have a variety of Western and Nepali dishes, and they have a great selection of beer and wine.

**Rating:** 4.0/5.0

*"In Kathmandu, the rhythm of life beats to the melodies of prayer flags and the echoes of ancient mantras."*

***- Manjushree Thapa***

# Chapter 8: Recreational and Fun Activities

Kathmandu, a city brimming with cultural wonders, also holds the key to a myriad of recreational and fun activities that cater to every traveler's desires and budget.

This chapter will unlock the thrilling experiences that await you, ensuring your visit to Kathmandu is filled with excitement and unforgettable memories.

## Hiking Trails:

Lace up your shoes and unlock the beauty of Kathmandu's surrounding hills with invigorating hiking trails.

Whether you opt for the popular Chandragiri Hills or choose off-the-beaten-path routes. Each hike promises breathtaking views of the city and the majestic Himalayan peaks.

## Cultural Workshops:

Immerse yourself in the city's rich cultural heritage by unlocking traditional workshops. Learn the art of Thangka painting, pottery, or dance, as local experts share their knowledge, offering an authentic experience of Nepal's artistic traditions.

## Bicycle Tours:

Pedal your way through the city's vibrant neighborhoods and unlock the hidden gems of Kathmandu on a bicycle tour. Experience the local way of life, encounter ancient temples, and enjoy the thrill of exploring the city on two wheels.

## Boating at Phewa Lake:

Unlock a serene escape by visiting Phewa Lake in nearby Pokhara. Rent a rowboat or a colorful paddle boat, and experience the tranquility of the lake surrounded by lush hills and the reflection of the Annapurna Range.

## Paragliding Adventure:

For the daring souls, unlock an adrenaline-pumping paragliding experience in the scenic Pokhara Valley. Soar like a bird above Phewa Lake and the picturesque landscape, capturing breathtaking aerial views that will leave you in awe.

## Yoga and Meditation Retreats:

Embark on a journey of self-discovery and unlock inner peace with yoga and meditation retreats offered in and around Kathmandu. Let expert instructors guide you through transformative practices, allowing you to recharge and find serenity amidst the bustling city.

## Visit to Swayambhunath Stupa:

Unlock spiritual bliss with a visit to the Swayambhunath Stupa, also known as the Monkey Temple. Climb the ancient steps and be rewarded with panoramic views of Kathmandu Valley while observing the playful monkeys that reside here.

# The 10 Best Things To Do In Kathmandu

**1. Visit the Durbar Squares:**

The Durbar Squares are a UNESCO World Heritage Site and are home to a number of temples, palaces, and courtyards. They are a great place to

**2. See Swayambhunath Stupa:**

Swayambhunath Stupa is a 500-year-old Buddhist stupa that is one of the most important religious sites in Nepal. It is located on a hilltop overlooking Kathmandu Valley and offers stunning views of the city.

**3. Go trekking in the Himalayas:**

If you are looking for an adventure, you can go trekking in the Himalayas. There are many different trekking trails to choose from, ranging from easy to difficult.

**4. Visit Pashupatinath Temple:**

Pashupatinath Temple is a Hindu temple dedicated to Shiva, the Hindu god of destruction and regeneration. It is one of the most important pilgrimage sites in Nepal.

5. **Explore Thamel:**

Thamel is a bustling neighborhood in Kathmandu that is home to many shops, restaurants, and cafes. It is a great place to experience Nepali culture and to shop for souvenirs.

6. **Take a cooking class:**

Nepali cuisine is delicious and diverse. There are many cooking classes in Kathmandu that can teach you how to make traditional Nepali dishes.

7. **Visit the Garden of Dreams:**

The Garden of Dreams is a beautiful garden that was built in the 19th century. It is a great place to relax and escape the hustle and bustle of Kathmandu.

8. **Go whitewater rafting:**

Whitewater rafting is a great way to experience the excitement of the rapids. There are a number of rafting companies in Kathmandu that offer rafting trips on the Trisuli River.

### 9. Go skydiving:

Skydiving is a once-in-a-lifetime experience that will give you amazing views of Kathmandu and the surrounding mountains. There are a number of skydiving companies in Kathmandu that offer skydiving trips.

- **Everest Skydive Nepal**

**Email:** nepal@everestskydive.com

**Webiste:** https://www.everestskydive.com/

### 10. Spend time with the locals:

The people of Kathmandu are friendly and welcoming. Make an effort to spend time with them and learn about their culture.

# The 10 Best Romantic Getaways for Couples in Kathmandu

1. **Garden Serenity:**

Unlock the romance of nature at the Garden of Dreams. With its lush lawns, blooming flowers, and serene ponds, this oasis unlocks an intimate setting for couples to unwind, stroll hand in hand, and enjoy whispered conversations.

2. **Sunset Splendor:**

Unlock the magic of sunset at Nagarkot. This hill station offers panoramic vistas that unlock a breathtaking canvas of colors as the sun sets behind the Himalayan peaks. Share this awe-inspiring moment as you cozy up and watch the sky unlock its beauty.

3. **Candlelit Dinners:**

Immerse yourselves in an enchanting dining experience by unlocking candlelit dinners. From upscale restaurants to cozy cafes, these intimate settings unlock the perfect ambiance to savor delectable meals and unlock heartfelt conversations.

**4. Rooftop Romance:**

Elevate your romance by unlocking the charm of rooftop dining. With the city's lights as a backdrop, unlock the joy of sharing a meal while soaking in the captivating views that Kathmandu's skyline has to offer.

**5. Historic Hideaways:**

Unlock the allure of Bhaktapur's ancient streets. Wander hand in hand, exploring age-old courtyards, intricate temples, and charming alleys that unlock the essence of romance amidst rich cultural heritage.

**6. Spa Escapes:**

Unlock relaxation and rejuvenation with a couple's spa experience. Unlock the tension as skilled hands pamper you both, unlocking a tranquil haven where you can unwind and cherish each other's company.

**7. Lakeside Bliss:**

Unlock the romance of Phewa Lake in Pokhara. Embark on a boat ride as the serene waters unlock a picturesque backdrop for stolen glances, shared laughter, and quiet moments of togetherness.

**8. Cultural Connections:**

Immerse yourselves in the city's cultural heritage by unlocking traditional performances. From classical music to dance shows, these experiences unlock a deeper connection as you appreciate Kathmandu's artistic soul.

**9. Picnic Retreats:**

Unlock a simple yet charming experience by having a romantic picnic. Choose a scenic spot like Godavari Botanical Garden, spread a blanket, and unlock the joy of sharing a meal in nature's embrace.

**10. Local Love:**

Unlock authenticity by partaking in local activities together. Unlock the fun of bargaining at markets, trying your hand at cooking traditional dishes, or participating in a local festival, creating memories that will forever unlock a special bond.

*"In Kathmandu, the air is filled with dreams, carried by the winds that whisper tales of ancient glory and future possibilities."*

***- Narayan Wagle***

# Chapter 9: Shopping Activities in Kathmandu

Kathmandu is a shopper's paradise, with something to offer everyone, regardless of their budget. From traditional handicrafts to modern souvenirs, you're sure to find something you love in this vibrant city.

In this chapter, we'll explore some of the best shopping destinations in Kathmandu, for all budgets. We'll also provide tips on how to get the best deals and avoid tourist traps.

## Shopping in Kathmandu for a low budget

If you're on a tight budget, don't worry, you can still find great deals on souvenirs and gifts in Kathmandu.

- **Thamel:**

This is the most popular tourist area in Kathmandu, and it's home to a wide variety of shops selling everything from souvenirs to trekking gear. You can find some great deals here, but be prepared to bargain hard.

- **Pashupatinath Temple flea market:**

This is a great place to find unique souvenirs and handicrafts. The prices are very reasonable, and you can often find one-of-a-kind items.

- **Kumaripati Handicraft Center:**

This government-run center sells a variety of high-quality handicrafts, including carpets, pottery, and jewelry. The prices are a bit higher than at the flea market, but the quality is guaranteed.

## Shopping in Kathmandu for a medium budget

If you have a bit more money to spend, you can still find great deals on shopping in Kathmandu.

- **Durbar Marg:**

This is the main shopping street in Kathmandu, and it's home to a number of high-end stores selling clothes, jewelry, and electronics.

- **Naya Bazaar:**

This is a newer shopping district that's home to a variety of stores selling clothes, shoes, and accessories. The prices are a bit higher than in Thamel, but the selection is better.

- **Kathmandu Durbar Square:**

This UNESCO World Heritage Site is home to a number of shops selling traditional handicrafts, including masks, puppets, and musical instruments. The prices are a bit higher than in Thamel, but the quality is excellent.

## Shopping in Kathmandu for a high budget

If you're looking to splurge, there are a number of high-end stores in Kathmandu that sell designer clothes, jewelry, and watches.

- **The Mall:**

This is a modern shopping mall with a number of high-end stores, including Zara, H&M, and Marks & Spencer.

- **Durbarmarg:**

This street is home to a number of high-end boutiques selling clothes, jewelry, and accessories.

- **Kamala Boutique:**

This store sells high-quality pashmina shawls, scarves, and other textiles.

# 4 Key Tips for Shopping in Kathmandu

1. **Bargain hard:**

This is especially important if you're shopping in Thamel or at the flea market. Don't be afraid to offer half the asking price, and be prepared to walk away if you don't get a good deal.

2. **Shop around:**

Compare prices before you buy anything. There are often big price differences between different stores, even for the same item.

3. **Be aware of tourist traps:**

There are a number of stores in Kathmandu that target tourists and overcharge them for souvenirs and gifts. Be sure to do your research before you buy anything.

4. **Be careful with your belongings:**

Kathmandu is a crowded city, and pickpockets are common. Be sure to keep your valuables close to you at all times.

*"In Kathmandu, the mountains become more than a backdrop; they become a part of your soul, forever etched in your memories."*

***- Rabi Thapa***

# Chapter 10:
# Language and Communication

Kathmandu is a diverse city with a mix of cultures and languages. The official language of Nepal is ***Nepali***, but English is also widely spoken, especially in tourist areas.

For a conducive and comfortable stay in Kathmandu, it's a good idea to learn a few basic Nepali phrases. This will help you communicate with locals and get around the city more easily.

## Nepali Language

Nepali is an Indo-Aryan language that is spoken by over 25 million people in Nepal and India. It is a tonal language, which means that the meaning of a word can change depending on the tone of voice used.

Nepali is written in the Devanagari script, which is also used for Hindi.

## English Language

English is widely spoken in Kathmandu, especially in tourist areas. Most hotels, restaurants, and shops have English-speaking staff. You will also find English newspapers and magazines available in Kathmandu.

## Unlocking Nepali Greetings:

Begin your journey by unlocking the power of greetings. ***"Namaste"*** is the key phrase that unlocks respect and warmth. Unlock this traditional greeting with a slight bow and folded hands, unlocking a sense of connection with the locals.

## Language Basics:

Immerse yourself in the Nepali language by unlocking a few essential phrases. Unlock gratitude with "Dhanyabad" (thank you) and unlock polite requests by saying "Kripaya" (please). These simple phrases unlock a friendly approach and appreciation for the local culture.

## Cultural Etiquette:

Remove your shoes before entering homes and sacred places. Remove your hat when entering religious sites, unlocking a gesture of respect for Nepal's traditions.

## Market Magic:

Unlock your bargaining skills with market vendors. Engage in friendly haggling by saying "Ali ghatau" (Please reduce the price a little) to unlock a potential discount while respecting the transaction.

## Understanding Numbers:

Unlock prices by asking "Kati ho?" (How much is it?) and unlock your understanding of quantities by learning numbers like "Ek" (one), "Dui" (two), and so on.

## Language Apps:

Unlock modern tools by using language apps. These apps unlock instant translations, making communication smoother and more accessible, allowing you to unlock deeper interactions.

## Common Phrases and Expressions:

When exploring Kathmandu, knowing a few common phrases and expressions can enhance your interactions with locals and make your trip more enjoyable. In this section, we will provide you with essential phrases for various situations, helping you navigate the city with ease.

### 28 Common Expression and Phrases To Connect Like a Pro

### Greetings and Basic Phrases

1. **Namaste (pronounced na-ma-stay)** - This is the traditional Nepali greeting. It is a gesture of respect and goodwill.
2. **Namaskar (pronounced na-ma-skar)** - This is another traditional Nepali greeting. It is similar to Namaste, but it is more formal.
3. **How are you? - Timi huncha?** (pronounced tee-mee hun-cha)
4. **I am fine. - Malai ramro cha.** (pronounced ma-lai ram-ro cha)

5. **Thank you. - Dhanyabaad.** (pronounced dhan-ya-baad)
6. **You're welcome. - Swagat ho.** (pronounced swa-gat ho)
7. **Excuse me. - Kina?** (pronounced kee-na)
8. **Sorry. - Ma maaf garchu.** (pronounced ma ma-af gar-chu)
9. **Goodbye. - Namaste.** (pronounced na-ma-stay)

## Ordering Food and Drinks

10. **I would like to order. - Ma khana lina chahanchu.** (pronounced ma khana li-na cha-han-chu)
11. **What do you recommend? - Timi ko yo thau ma kei ramro khana cha?** (pronounced tee-mee ko yo thau ma kee ram-ro khana cha?)
12. **Can I have the menu? - Menu deu na.** (pronounced me-nu deu na)
13. **I would like a glass of water. - Malai pani ko glass hana.** (pronounced ma-lai pa-ni ko glaas ha-na)
14. **I would like a cup of coffee. - Malai coffee ko cup hana.** (pronounced ma-lai ko-fee ko cup ha-na)

15. **I would like a beer. - Malai beer hana.** (pronounced ma-lai beer ha-na)

## Asking for Directions

16. **Excuse me, can you help me? - Kina? Timi nagari ma kaha janu paryo?** (pronounced kee-na? tee-mee na-ga-ri ma ka-ha ja-nu par-yo?)
17. **How do I get to the [place]? - Malai [place] jan ne batti deu na.** (pronounced ma-lai [place] jan ne bat-ti deu na)
18. **Is it far? - Kati dur cha?** (pronounced ka-ti dur cha?)
19. **Can you show me on the map? - Map ma dekhau na.** (pronounced map ma dek-hau na)

## Shopping and Bargaining

20. **How much is this? - Yo kati ho?** (pronounced yo ka-ti ho?)
21. **Can you give me a discount? - Discount dinu huncha?** (pronounced dis-count di-nu hun-cha?)
22. **That's too expensive. - Yo bahut mahago cha.** (pronounced yo bahut ma-ha-go cha)

23. **What is your best price? - Timi ko best price kati ho?** (pronounced tee-mee ko best price ka-ti ho?)
24. **I will pay [price]. - Malai [price] ma kinnu cha.** (pronounced ma-lai [price] ma kin-nu cha)

## Expressing Gratitude

25. **Thank you. - Dhanyabaad.** (pronounced dhan-ya-baad)
26. **You're welcome. - Swagat ho.** (pronounced swa-gat ho)
27. **I appreciate it. - Malai yo man paryo.** (pronounced ma-lai yo man par-yo)
28. **You have helped me a lot. - Timi le malai bahut sahayata gareu.** (pronounced tee-mee le ma-lai bahut sa-ha-ya-ta ga-reu)

## 4 Key Tips for Communicating Like A Pro

1. Learn a few basic Nepali phrases. This will help you communicate with locals and get around the city more easily.
2. If you don't know a Nepali phrase, try speaking English. Most people in Kathmandu will understand basic English.
3. Be patient. Communication can be slow in Kathmandu, especially if you are speaking with someone who doesn't speak English well.
4. Be respectful. Nepali culture is very different from Western culture. Be sure to be respectful of local customs and traditions.

*"Kathmandu, a city that embraces you with warmth and kindness, making you feel like a cherished guest in its timeless embrace."*

***- Laura Jean McKay***

# Chapter 11: Essential Information

Kathmandu being the capital of Nepal and a popular tourist destination. It is a city with a rich history and culture, and there are many things to see and do. As you are planning a trip to Kathmandu, there are a few essential things you need to know.

## Visas and Currency

Citizens of most countries need a visa to enter Nepal. You can apply for a visa at the Nepali embassy or consulate in your home country. The currency of Nepal is the Nepalese rupee (NPR). You can exchange your currency for NPR at banks, currency exchange bureaus, and hotels.

## Transportation

The best way to get around Kathmandu is by walking or taking a taxi. There are also a few buses that run within the city. If you are planning on doing any hiking or trekking, you will need to hire a car or a jeep.

## Accommodation

There are a variety of accommodation options available in Kathmandu, from budget hostels to luxury hotels. If you are on a budget, you can find a hostel for around $10 per night. If you are looking for something more luxurious, you can find a hotel for around $100 per night.

## Safety

Kathmandu is generally a safe city, but it is important to be aware of your surroundings. There have been reports of petty theft, so it is important to keep your valuables close to you. It is also a good idea to avoid walking around alone at night.

## Health

The tap water in Kathmandu is not safe to drink. You should drink bottled water or boil the tap water before drinking it. You should also be aware of the risk of altitude sickness if you are planning on doing any hiking or trekking.

## Culture and Etiquette

Nepal is a multi-cultural country, and there are many different religions and customs practiced. It is important to be respectful of local customs and traditions.

For example, it is considered polite to remove your shoes before entering a temple or a home. It is also polite to dress modestly, especially when visiting religious sites.

## Emergency Situations

- If you are in an emergency, dial 100 for the police or 102 for the ambulance.
- You can also call the tourist police at +977-1-4108021.
- If you are lost, ask a local for help. They will be happy to assist you.

*"In Kathmandu, you don't just visit a place; you immerse yourself in a way of life that touches your soul and transforms your perspective."*

***- Lisa Choegyal***

# Frequently Asked Questions (FAQ)

In your quest to unlock the wonders of Kathmandu, having answers to common questions can transform your journey into a smoother and more enjoyable experience. This chapter unlocks the FAQs that provide clarity and confidence as you embark on your adventure.

**Q1: Do I need a visa to enter Kathmandu?**

**A:** Yes, most visitors require a visa to enter Nepal. Unlock convenience by obtaining a visa-on-arrival at the airport or land borders.

**Q2: What currency is used in Kathmandu?**

**A:** The currency used is the Nepalese Rupee (NPR). Unlock ATMs for easy currency exchange and card payments in various establishments.

**Q3: How do I get around the city?**

**A:** Unlock various transportation options. Unlock local buses, taxis, and rickshaws for shorter distances and unlock navigating with local maps or apps.

**Q4: Is English widely spoken?**

**A:** Yes, English is commonly spoken, especially in urban areas. Unlock the ability to communicate and unlock interactions with locals.

**Q5: What's the best time to visit Kathmandu?**

**A:** Unlock a pleasant journey by visiting during spring (March to May) and autumn (September to November). Unlock favorable weather for exploration.

**Q6: Can I bargain while shopping?**

**A:** Yes, bargaining is common in markets. Unlock your negotiation skills to unlock a good deal on handicrafts, textiles, and souvenirs.

**Q7: What should I wear when visiting temples?**

**A:** Unlock respect by dressing modestly. Unlock covering your shoulders and knees, and unlock removing shoes before entering sacred places.

**Q8: Are there any health precautions I should take?**

**A:** Unlock good health by drinking bottled or boiled water. Unlock carrying basic medications and being cautious with street food.

**Q9: What are the must-try local dishes?**

**A:** Unlock culinary delights by trying momos (dumplings), dal bhat (rice and lentil dish), and traditional Newari cuisine.

**Q10: How do I show respect to locals?**

**A:** Unlock cultural appreciation by using polite phrases like "Namaste." Unlock respect for elders by addressing them as "Dai" (brother) or "Didi" (sister).

**Q11: Are there any cultural taboos I should be aware of?**

**A:** Unlock cultural awareness by avoiding public displays of affection. Unlock respect by not pointing your feet at people or religious objects.

**Q12: Can I hike or trek around Kathmandu?**

**A:** Yes, you can. Unlock the adventure of hiking or trekking in nearby hills like Nagarkot and Shivapuri, unlocking stunning vistas.

In a nutshell, this FAQ section unlocks insights that ensure your journey in Kathmandu is as smooth as possible. Whether you're unlocking visa information, health precautions, or cultural norms, each answer unlocks a foundation for an enriched experience.

*"Kathmandu, a city that captivates your heart, opens your mind, and nourishes your spirit with its timeless wisdom."*

***- Sienna Craig***

# The Ideal 7-Days Itinerary Plan in Kathmandu

In this section, we present an ideal 7-day itinerary that encompasses the best attractions and experiences this enchanting destination has to offer.

## Day 1: Arrive in Kathmandu

- Arrive in Kathmandu and check into your hotel.

- Visit Durbar Square, a UNESCO World Heritage Site and home to a number of temples and palaces.

- Take a walk around Thamel, the tourist hub of Kathmandu, and do some shopping.

- Enjoy a traditional Nepali dinner at a local restaurant.

## Day 2: Visit Pashupatinath Temple

- Visit Pashupatinath Temple, one of the holiest Hindu temples in Nepal.

- Take a boat ride on the Bagmati River and see the cremations that take place along the banks.

- Visit Swayambhunath Temple, a Buddhist temple that is also known as the Monkey Temple.

## Day 3: Take a day trip to Nagarkot

- Take a day trip to Nagarkot, a beautiful hilltop town with stunning views of the Himalayas.

- Go hiking or trekking in the surrounding area.

- Enjoy a picnic lunch with a view.

## Day 4: Visit Bhaktapur

- Visit Bhaktapur, a UNESCO World Heritage Site and one of the three ancient cities of the Kathmandu Valley.

- Explore the maze of streets and alleyways, and see the many temples and palaces.

- Learn about Bhaktapur's unique culture and traditions.

## Day 5: Visit Patan

- Visit Patan, another UNESCO World Heritage Site and the third ancient city of the Kathmandu Valley.

- See the many temples and palaces, including the Golden Temple.

- Shop for souvenirs and handicrafts in the Patan Durbar Square area.

## Day 6: Visit the Pashupatinath Museum

- Visit the Pashupatinath Museum, which houses a collection of artifacts from Pashupatinath Temple.
- Learn about the history and culture of Pashupatinath Temple.
- Take a cooking class and learn how to make traditional Nepali dishes.

## Day 7: Departure

- Relax at your hotel or go for a final walk around Thamel.
- Have a farewell dinner at a nice restaurant.
- Catch your flight back home.

# Final Thoughts

As your journey through this travel guide to Kathmandu comes to an end, we hope that you have found it informative and inspiring. Kathmandu is a destination that captures the hearts of travelers with its breathtaking views, rich history, and warm hospitality.

I hope this travel guide has inspired you to visit Kathmandu soon. If you do, I'm sure you'll have a wonderful time.

***Here are a few final thoughts to keep in mind when planning your trip to Kathmandu:***

- **Be flexible with your itinerary.**

Things don't always go according to plan in Kathmandu, so it's important to be flexible with your itinerary. If there's a temple that's closed for repairs, or if there's a traffic jam, don't be afraid to change your plans.

- **Be patient.**

Kathmandu is a crowded city, and things move slowly. Be patient with the locals, and don't get frustrated if things don't happen as quickly as you'd like.

- **Be respectful of local customs and traditions.**

Nepal is a multi-cultural country, and there are many different religions and customs practiced. Be respectful of local customs and traditions, and avoid doing anything that might be offensive.

- **Have fun!**

Kathmandu is a great city to visit, and you're sure to have a lot of fun. Explore the temples and palaces, go hiking in the mountains, and try some of the delicious Nepali food.

We hope that this travel guide has provided you with the knowledge and inspiration to embark on a remarkable adventure in Kathmandu, where every street corner reveals a new story and every moment becomes a treasure to cherish.

Safe travels, and may your future journeys be filled with the same wonder and delight you've experienced in Kathmandu.

Until we meet again,

***Dan L. Allbeta***

# Travel Journal

## Travel Budget

# Travel Budget

| | Transportation | Food | Accommodation |
|---|---|---|---|
| Budget | | | |

| | Shopping | Subscription | Entertainment |
|---|---|---|---|
| Budget | | | |

# Packing Checklist

# Packing Checklist

| Documents | Clothes | Toiletries |
| --- | --- | --- |
| | | |

| Gadgets | Contacts | Miscellaneous |
| --- | --- | --- |
| | | |

# Travel Itinerary

# Travel Itinerary

## Day 1

| Place To See | | |
|---|---|---|
| Transportation | Activity | Time |
| | | |

## Day 2

| Place To See | | |
|---|---|---|
| Transportation | Activity | Time |
| | | |

# Travel Itinerary

## Day 3

| Place To See | | |
|---|---|---|
| Transportation | Activity | Time |
| | | |
| | | |
| | | |
| | | |
| | | |
| | | |

## Day 4

| Place To See | | |
|---|---|---|
| Transportation | Activity | Time |
| | | |
| | | |
| | | |
| | | |
| | | |
| | | |

# Travel Itinerary

## Day 5

| Place To See | | |
|---|---|---|
| Transportation | Activity | Time |

## Day 6

| Place To See | | |
|---|---|---|
| Transportation | Activity | Time |

# Travel Itinerary

## Day 7

| Place To See | | |
|---|---|---|
| Transportation | Activity | Time |
| | | |
| | | |
| | | |
| | | |
| | | |
| | | |
| | | |

## Day 8

| Place To See | | |
|---|---|---|
| Transportation | Activity | Time |
| | | |
| | | |
| | | |
| | | |
| | | |
| | | |
| | | |

# Travel Itinerary

## Day 9

| Place To See | | |
|---|---|---|
| Transportation | Activity | Time |
| | | |
| | | |
| | | |
| | | |
| | | |
| | | |

## Day 10

| Place To See | | |
|---|---|---|
| Transportation | Activity | Time |
| | | |
| | | |
| | | |
| | | |
| | | |
| | | |

# My Notes

# My Note

# My Note

# My Note

# My Note

# My Note

# My Note

# My Note

# My Note

# My Note

# My Note

# My Note

Printed in Great Britain
by Amazon

58729125R00076